FEEL-DEAL-HEAL

Acquiring LOVE - Liberty Over Vulnerable Emotions

JOURNAL

DR. LATOSHIA DANIELS

FEEL-DEAL-HEAL

This journal belongs to: _______________________________________

Date: ____________________

Dear Journal Owner,

I hope this letter finds you in a moment of openness and willingness to embark on a journey of profound self-discovery and healing. As the bearer of this journal, you hold within your hands a powerful tool for transformation - "Feel. Deal. Heal.: Acquiring L.O.V.E. - Liberty Over Vulnerable Emotions."

In the pages of this journal, you will discover a pathway to reclaiming your joy, one that is rooted in the principles outlined in the companion book, "Feel-Deal-Heal: Acquiring LOVE – Liberty Over Vulnerable Emotions." This isn't just another journal; it's a sacred space for personal exploration, emotional intelligence, and spiritual growth.

As humans, we are blessed with the capacity to feel a vast array of emotions, each one shaping our interactions with the world and with ourselves. Yet, all too often, we find ourselves avoiding those emotions that make us feel vulnerable or uncomfortable. We push them aside, burying them deep within ourselves, or erecting walls of protection to shield us from their impact.

But here's the truth: by ignoring our emotional discomfort, we only perpetuate our own suffering. We carry around emotional baggage that weighs us down, chains that bind us, and walls that block out the very goodness we seek in life. And in doing so, we become resentful, intolerable, distrustful, and more.

That's where "Feel. Deal. Heal." comes in. This journal is your invitation to break free from the shackles of emotional repression and embrace a life of authenticity and liberation. Through a series of writing prompts, each corresponding to a letter of love from the book, you will embark on a journey of self-discovery and healing unlike any other.

As you journey through these prompts, may you find the courage to confront your vulnerabilities, the strength to embrace your emotions, and the wisdom to heal and grow. This journal is your companion on the path to acquiring L.O.V.E. - Liberty Over Vulnerable Emotions.

With heartfelt wishes for your journey,

Grow in love,

Dr. Latoshia

Dr. Latoshia

Feel-Deal-Heal Process

Feel: Identify the feelings/emotions associated with the hurtful or painful event and feel them.

Deal: Actively seek resolution, make decisions, and implement strategies to manage and mitigate the impact of the event on your emotions and well-being.

Heal: Nurture self, practice self-compassion, and engage in activities that promote healing and growth. Move beyond pain and towards a sense of wholeness and inner peace.

HOW TO USE THE JOURNAL

Song of the Day: Start your journaling session by identifying a song that resonates with you and helps bring you to a place of peace, and calm, or prompts positive emotions, thoughts, and feelings. Take a few moments to listen to this song, allowing its melody and lyrics to uplift your spirit and set a positive tone for your journaling experience. You can jot down the title of the song and a brief note about why you chose it, reflecting on the emotions it evokes and how it influences your mood.

Mood: Next, take a moment to check in with yourself and identify your current mood. Consider how you're feeling emotionally and mentally in this present moment. You can use descriptive words such as "happy," "sad," "anxious," or "content" to articulate your mood. This simple exercise helps you become more aware of your emotional state and provides a starting point for your journaling journey.

Energy Level: Assess your energy level by noting how physically energized or fatigued you feel. Rate your energy level on a scale from 1 to 10, with 1 being deficient energy and 10 being extremely high energy. Pay attention to any factors that may be influencing your energy levels, such as sleep quality, physical activity, or stress levels. This self-awareness can help you make intentional choices throughout the day to manage your energy more effectively.

Mindset: Reflect on your current mindset and the quality of your thoughts. Are your thoughts predominantly positive, negative, or neutral? Do you notice any recurring patterns or themes in your thinking? Consider how your mindset influences your mood, behavior, and overall well-being. You can use this space to challenge negative thoughts and cultivate a more positive and resilient mindset through affirmations, gratitude, and self-reflection.

Gratitude: Take a moment to express gratitude for the blessings and positive experiences in your life. Write down three things you're grateful for, no matter how big or small. Cultivating a practice of gratitude can help shift your focus from what's lacking to what's abundant in your life, fostering a sense of appreciation and contentment. Regularly acknowledging and savoring moments of gratitude can contribute to greater happiness and well-being over time.

Prayer: Dedicate a section of your journal to prayer or spiritual reflection. Use this space to connect with your God, express your hopes, concerns, and desires, or simply offer words of thanks and praise. Prayer can be a powerful tool for finding peace, guidance, and solace in times of need. Write down your prayers or thoughts, allowing yourself to be open and vulnerable in your communication with the Divine.

By incorporating these components into your journaling practice, you can enhance your self-awareness, cultivate positive emotions, and promote overall emotional well-being. Remember that journaling is a personal and flexible process, so feel free to adapt these components to suit your individual preferences and needs.

Rating your energy level from 1 to 10 allows you to assess how energized and motivated you feel at a given moment. You can gain insight into how you're feeling physically and mentally, allowing you to adjust your activities and self-care practices accordingly. It's a simple yet effective way to tune into your body and optimize your daily performance and well-being. Here's a quick breakdown:

1. **Low Energy (1-3):** Feeling extremely fatigued, lethargic, and unable to engage in activities.

2. **Moderate Energy (4-6):** Experiencing some energy but not at peak levels. You may feel a bit tired but still able to function.

3. **High Energy (7-9):** Feeling energized, alert, and ready to tackle tasks with enthusiasm.

4. **Peak Energy (10):** Experiencing maximum energy and vitality, feeling fully awake, alert, and ready for anything.

Date: _________ Time:________ Mood: ________ Energy Level:________ Mindset: __________

Song of the day: ____

I am grateful for...

1.

2.

3.

Letter of Love 1

How can I enhance my emotional intelligence to better handle emotional injuries and challenges in the future? Are there specific areas, such as self-awareness, empathy, and self-regulation, that I can focus on improving to strengthen my emotional well-being and resilience?

Prayer:

Date: _________ Time:________ Mood: _________ Energy Level:________ Mindset: __________

Song of the day: ____

I am grateful for…

1.

2.

3.

Letter of Love 2

How do I assess my mental and emotional health and well-being? What habits and practices contribute to my mental and emotional stability, and how can I improve and maintain it over time?

Prayer:

Date: ________ Time:________ Mood: ________ Energy Level:________ Mindset: __________

Song of the day: ____

I am grateful for...

1.

2.

3.

Letter of Love 3:

How have damaged roots affected my relationships, self-perception, and overall well-being? What steps can I take to address and heal from emotional damage, both on my own and with the support of others?

Prayer:

Date: _________ Time:_________ Mood: _________ Energy Level:_________ Mindset: __________

Song of the day: ____

I am grateful for…

1.

2.

3.

Letter of Love 4

Identify three core beliefs. Are they positive or negative? What contributed to the negative beliefs (nature or nurture)? Am I willing to change negative core beliefs to enhance my emotional and social well-being?

Prayer:

Date: _________ Time:________ Mood: ________ Energy Level:________ Mindset: __________

Song of the day: ____

I am grateful for…

1.

2.

3.

Letter of Love 5:

What is the default emotion I use to protect myself from being hurt or vulnerable? Why that particular emotion? Has it impacted my self-perspective? Explain.

Prayer:

EQASSESSMENT

On a scale of 1-7, with 1= strongly disagree and 7 = strongly agree, answer the following questions.

I feel satisfied with the person I am right now. ___________ I do not allow regrets and disappointments to interfere with my day. __________ I am very connected with others and do not feel lonely. _______ I am generally a rational and optimistic thinker. _______ I refuse to hold grudges and can be forgiving. ________ I feel in control of my emotions, thoughts, speech, and actions. __________ I am grateful for how my life is currently without focusing on the lack. __________ I enjoy a healthy sense of humor and can laugh at life's shortcomings. _________

56-51 = Extraordinary 50-46 = High 45-40 = Moderate 39-32 = Needs a boost 31-34 = Needs attention 23-16 = Needs improvement 15 - below = Danger zone!

Total: _______________

Date: _________ Time:_________ Mood: _________ Energy Level:_________ Mindset: __________

Song of the day: ____

I am grateful for…

1.

2.

3.

Letter of Love 6:

What baggage am I carrying around that I need to unload? What will it take for me to drop the bags? Am I willing to give God all of my baggage?

Prayer:

Date: _________ Time:________ Mood: ________ Energy Level:________ Mindset: _________

Song of the day: ____

I am grateful for…

1.

2.

3.

Letter of Love 7:

What emotional walls have I built in my life, and how have they affected my relationships and well-being? What steps can I take to understand and break down the emotional walls I have constructed, allowing for deeper connections and personal growth?

Prayer:

Date: _________ Time:_________ Mood: _________ Energy Level:_________ Mindset: __________

Song of the day: ____

I am grateful for…

1.

2.

3.

Letter of Love 8:

How do I typically react to emotional rollercoasters, and what strategies have proven effective in helping me navigate these turbulent times? What lessons can I learn from past emotional rollercoasters to better cope with future challenges and maintain emotional balance?

Prayer:

Date: _________ Time:_________ Mood: _________ Energy Level:_________ Mindset: _________

Song of the day: ____

I am grateful for…

1.

2.

3.

Letter of Love 9:

In what ways have I felt emotionally imprisoned, and what specific thoughts or behaviors may be contributing to this sense of confinement? What steps can I take to free myself from emotional imprisonment and experience greater emotional freedom and well-being?

Prayer:

Date: _________ Time:_______ Mood: ________ Energy Level:_______ Mindset: _________

Song of the day: ____

I am grateful for…

1.

2.

3.

Letter of Love 10:

Write a letter to pain. Explain the impact it has on my life. Describe any strong emotions such as anger, regret, shame, guilt, bitterness, etc. that I carry. What are the roots of my emotional pain, and how can I better understand its origins and triggers? What are healthy ways I can process and heal?

Prayer:

Date: _________ Time:________ Mood: _________ Energy Level:________ Mindset: __________

Song of the day: ____

I am grateful for...

1.

2.

3.

Letter of Love 11:

How do I currently express love authentically in my relationships, and are there areas where I can improve in communicating my true feelings? Do I have problems demonstrating or accepting love? Why? What obstacles or fears might be preventing me from fully expressing 1 Corinthians 13:4-7 love?

Prayer:

Date: _________ Time:________ Mood: ________ Energy Level:________ Mindset: __________

Song of the day: ____

I am grateful for…

1.

2.

3.

Letter of Love 12:

How has tainted love impacted my emotional well-being, and what specific emotions or challenges have I experienced as a result? In what ways do I believe I can break free from the grasp of tainted love and prioritize my emotional well-being moving forward?

Prayer:

Date: _________ Time:_________ Mood: _________ Energy Level:_________ Mindset: __________

Song of the day: ____

I am grateful for…

1.

2.

3.

Letter of Love 13:

How can I cultivate a practice of self-love in my daily life, and what positive changes do I believe it will bring to my emotional well-being and healing journey?

Prayer:

Date: _________ Time:_________ Mood: _________ Energy Level:_________ Mindset: __________

Song of the day: ____

I am grateful for...

1.

2.

3.

Letter of Love 14:

Where do I make the majority of my emotional deposits? What standards and requirements have I developed so that others understand and know my worth?

Prayer:

Date: _________ Time:_________ Mood: _________ Energy Level:_________ Mindset: __________

Song of the day: ____

I am grateful for…

1.

2.

3.

Letter of Love 15:

When someone offers to help me, do I question their motives? Do I have difficulty trusting others? If so why? How well do I receive input from those who love and care about me?

Prayer:

Date: _________ Time:________ Mood: ________ Energy Level:________ Mindset: __________

Song of the day: ____

I am grateful for...

1.

2.

3.

Letter of Love 16:

    When I am upset what do I do? What has my anger cost me? Is there a particular situation, experience, or person I am angry about or with? Explain. How long have I held onto this feeling? Why?

Prayer:

Date: _________ Time:________ Mood: ________ Energy Level:________ Mindset: _________

Song of the day: ____

I am grateful for…

1.

2.

3.

Letter of Love 16:

When I am upset what do I do? What has my anger cost me? Is there a particular situation, experience, or person I am angry about or with? Explain. How long have I held onto this feeling? Why?

Prayer:

Things I Can and Can't Control

Identify things you cannot control for the black heart.

Identify things you can control for the white heart.

ANGER

What is the root cause?

Many individuals' anger often stems from either pain or fear. Take a moment to recognize and acknowledge the sources of pain and fear in your life that might be fueling your feelings of anger.

PAIN   **FEAR**

Date: _________ Time:_______ Mood: ________ Energy Level:_______ Mindset: _________

Song of the day: ____

I am grateful for…

1.

2.

3.

Letter of Love 17:

Have I experienced a significant loss in my life, and if so, how has my journey through grief and healing impacted my understanding of resilience and the impermanence of life? What emotions do I feel regarding unaddressed grief and how do I display them?

Prayer:

Date: _________ Time:_________ Mood: _________ Energy Level:_________ Mindset: __________

Song of the day: ____

I am grateful for...

1.

2.

3.

Letter of Love 18:

What self-care practices or sources of support can I implement to help in my process of overcoming grief and emotional wounds associated with loss? How can the strategies influence my healing and personal growth?

Prayer:

Date: _________ Time:________ Mood: _________ Energy Level:________ Mindset: __________

Song of the day: ____

I am grateful for…

1.

2.

3.

Letter of Love 19:

Am I taking responsibility for my actions and decisions, or am I inclined to blame others? how can I better hold myself accountable for my choices? When faced with situations where others are wrong am I quick to accept blame to keep the peace? How can I assertively address such instances without taking undue responsibility?

Prayer:

Date: _________ Time:_________ Mood: _________ Energy Level:_________ Mindset: __________

Song of the day: ____

I am grateful for…

1.

2.

3.

Letter of Love 20:

What has me mentally or emotionally bound? What negative or self-limiting thoughts have generated from the bondage? How can you use what broke you to help you and others? Explain.

Prayer:

Date: _________ Time:_______ Mood: ________ Energy Level:_______ Mindset: _________

Song of the day: ____

I am grateful for…

1.

2.

3.

Letter of Love 21:

What secrets or unspoken truths have I been carrying that may be contributing to my emotional wounds, and how have they affected my well-being? What steps can I take to address and heal from the emotional wounds tied to these secrets, and what support or strategies might I need to navigate this process?

Prayer:

Date: _________ Time:_________ Mood: _________ Energy Level:_________ Mindset: __________

Song of the day: ____

I am grateful for...

1.

2.

3.

Letter of Love 22:

How do I typically react when strong emotions arise, and are these reactions serving my well-being and relationships positively? What strategies or coping methods can I develop to better manage and harness strong emotions constructively, rather than being overwhelmed by them?

Prayer:

Date: _________ Time:________ Mood: ________ Energy Level:________ Mindset: __________

Song of the day: ____

I am grateful for…

1.

2.

3.

Letter of Love 23:

How do I typically react when strong emotions arise, and are these reactions serving my well-being and relationships positively? What has my lack of control cost me? What strategies or coping methods can I develop to better manage and harness strong emotions constructively, rather than being overwhelmed by them?

Prayer:

Date: _________ Time:_________ Mood: _________ Energy Level:_________ Mindset: __________

Song of the day: ____

I am grateful for…

1.

2.

3.

Letter of Love 24:

What life struggles am I currently facing, and how can I approach them with resilience and determination, acknowledging that the struggle is indeed real? In what ways can I find strength and growth amidst life's challenges, embracing the reality of struggle as a path to personal development and achievement?

Prayer:

Date: _________ Time:________ Mood: _________ Energy Level:________ Mindset: __________

Song of the day: ____

I am grateful for…

1.

2.

3.

Letter of Love 25:

How am I actively nurturing my emotional health and well-being on a regular basis, and are there signs that I might be approaching a breaking point? What preventive measures and self-care strategies can I implement to maintain a healthy emotional state and avoid reaching a breaking point in my life?

Prayer:

Date: _________ Time:________ Mood: ________ Energy Level:________ Mindset: _________

Song of the day: ____

I am grateful for…

1.

2.

3.

Letter of Love 26:

What coping methods have I found most effective in dealing with emotional discomfort, and how can I consistently apply them in challenging moments? Are there new coping strategies or techniques I can explore to enhance my ability to manage and navigate emotional discomfort in a healthier and more constructive manner?

Prayer:

Date: _________ Time:_________ Mood: _________ Energy Level:_________ Mindset: __________

Song of the day: ____

I am grateful for…

1.

2.

3.

Letter of Love 27:

What specific factors or situations are contributing to my feelings of hopelessness, and how can I begin to address them or seek support? In what ways can I cultivate a sense of hope, even int he face of difficult circumstances, and what positive steps can I take to regain a sense of purpose and optimism?

Prayer:

Date: _________ Time:________ Mood: ________ Energy Level:________ Mindset: __________

Song of the day: ____

I am grateful for…

1.

2.

3.

Letter of Love 28:

How have hurtful words from others impacted my emotional stability, and what self-care practices can I employ to heal from their effects? In what ways can I establish healthy boundaries and communicate assertively when confronted with hurtful words, fostering emotional stability and self-respect?

Prayer:

Date: _________ Time:________ Mood: ________ Energy Level:________ Mindset: _________

Song of the day: ____

I am grateful for…

1.

2.

3.

Letter of Love 29:

How do I currently perceive my self-worth and self-esteem, and what positive affirmations or practices can I incorporate to enhance these aspects of my self-image? Are there past experiences or beliefs that have been diminishing my self-worth, and what steps can I take to challenge and reframe these perceptions, fostering a healthier sense of self-esteem?

Prayer:

Date: _________ Time:_________ Mood: _________ Energy Level:_________ Mindset: __________

Song of the day: ____

I am grateful for…

1.

2.

3.

Letter of Love 30:

When was there a time in my life where I made the choice to stand with someone instead of abandoning them in hard times? Why did I make that choice? When was the last time someone was there for me during a hard time? Did I push them away or let them stay? Why?

Prayer:

Date: _________ Time:________ Mood: ________ Energy Level:________ Mindset: __________

Song of the day: ____

I am grateful for…

1.

2.

3.

Letter of Love 31:

What aspects of my temperament or reactions can I work on to enhance my resilience in the face of adversity, and how can I begin this process of self-improvement? In what ways can I actively cultivate resilience as a core trait, and what daily practices or strategies can help me grow stronger and more adaptable in the midst of life's challenges?

Prayer:

Date: _________ Time:________ Mood: ________ Energy Level:________ Mindset: _________

Song of the day: ____

I am grateful for…

1.

2.

3.

Letter of Love 32:

How do I feel about giving help to others, and am I open to receiving help when I need it? How can I create a more balanced and supportive dynamic in my relationships? What barriers or beliefs might be hindering my ability to ask for and accept help, and what steps can I take to become more open to receiving support while continuing to offer it to others?

Prayer:

Date: _________ Time:_________ Mood: _________ Energy Level:_________ Mindset: __________

Song of the day: ____

I am grateful for…

1.

2.

3.

Letter of Love 33:

How do I typically respond to negativity from haters, social media trolls, and unlovely individuals, and are there more constructive ways I can protect my emotional well-being and self-esteem in the face of their comments? In what ways can I develop resilience and inner strength to remain focused on my goals and well-being, rather than being negatively affected by the words of those who seek to bring me down?

Prayer:

Date: _________ Time:_________ Mood: _________ Energy Level:_________ Mindset: __________

Song of the day: ____

I am grateful for…

1.

2.

3.

Letter of Love 34:

What qualities do I value most in my friendships, and do my current friendships align with these values? How can I nurture these connections? Am I fostering a healthy balance between giving and receiving in my friendships, and what can I do to ensure that these relationships continue to be a source of support and joy for both me and my friends?

Prayer:

Date: __________ Time:_________ Mood: _________ Energy Level:_________ Mindset: __________

Song of the day: ____

I am grateful for…

1.

2.

3.

Letter of Love 35:

How can I step outside my current perspective and view the problems and challenges in my life through a fresh lens, and what new insights or solutions might this approach reveal? What strategies or practices can I employ to encourage a more open and adaptable mindset, enabling me to approach problems and challenges with a greater sense of creativity and resourcefulness?

Prayer:

Date: _________ Time:________ Mood: ________ Energy Level:________ Mindset: _________

Song of the day: ____

I am grateful for…

1.

2.

3.

Letter of Love 36:

What specific growth or valuable lessons have I experienced through the struggles and growing pains in my life, and how can I leverage these experiences for personal development? In what ways can I embrace the challenges and discomfort associated with growth, viewing them as opportunities for learning and transformation rather than mere obstacles?

Prayer:

Date: _________ Time:________ Mood: _________ Energy Level:________ Mindset: __________

Song of the day: ____

I am grateful for...

1.

2.

3.

Letter of Love 37:

Has my pain served a purpose or kept me from fulfilling my purpose? How can I use the pain of life woes as a catalyst for personal growth and a deeper connection to my life's purpose, rather than allowing it to hinder my progress? What strategies can I employ to transform the pain of life's challenges into a driving force that propels me toward my purpose, while maintaining resilience and determination?

Prayer:

Date: _________ Time:_________ Mood: _________ Energy Level:_________ Mindset: __________

Song of the day: ____

I am grateful for…

1.

2.

3.

Letter of Love 38:

What aspects of my true self have I been hiding behind a mask, and how can I courageously unveil these qualities to live a more authentic and fulfilling life?

Prayer:

Date: _________ Time:________ Mood: _________ Energy Level:________ Mindset: __________

Song of the day: ____

I am grateful for…

1.

2.

3.

Letter of Love 39:

In what ways have past experiences of hardship deepened my faith, and what strategies can I employ to continue to trust in the face of adversity, knowing that brighter days may lie ahead?

Prayer:

Date: _________ Time:_________ Mood: _________ Energy Level:_________ Mindset: __________

Song of the day: ____

I am grateful for…

1.

2.

3.

Letter of Love 40:

In what ways can I deepen my trust in God's guidance and find strength in the process of healing, recognizing that the person I am becoming is a testament to His love and purpose for my life?

Prayer: